Peafowls, Peacocks and Peahens

Facts and Information.

The Complete Owner's Guide.

The must have guide for anyone passionate about breeding, owning, keeping and raising peafowls or peacocks.
Including information and facts about: blue, white, Indian and green peacocks and peafowls.

by

Elliott Lang

Published by IMB Publishing
2013 Edition

With thanks to my dad for teaching me all about peacocks.

Also thanks to my wife and kids for sticking with me throughout the many hours I spent writing this book.

Table of Contents

CHAPTER ONE: INTRODUCTION 7

CHAPTER TWO: UNDERSTANDING PEACOCKS AND PEAFOWL 12

1) Short History of the Peacock 12
2) General Facts about Peafowl 14
3) Temperament of Peacocks and Peafowl 19

CHAPTER THREE: ARE YOU READY TO RAISE PEACOCKS AND PEAFOWLS 22

1) Pros and Cons of Owning Peafowl 25
2) Free Range or Penned 29

CHAPTER FOUR: CHOOSING THE RIGHT PEACOCK AND PEAFOWL .. 34

1) Types of Peafowl 34
   a) Species *35*
   b) Patterns *39*
   c) Colours *54*
2) Choosing Your Peafowl 62

CHAPTER FIVE: BRINGING YOUR BIRDS HOME 69

1) Special Permits 69
2) Pens and Housing 70
3) Building a Roost 73
4) Protection from Predators 74
5) Bringing the Peafowl Home 75

CHAPTER SIX: CARING FOR YOUR PEACOCK 77

1) Daily Care 77
2) Clipping the Wing 81
3) Wormers and Vaccinations 83
4) Administering Oral Medication 83
5) Administering Intramuscular Medication 85
6) Diseases 87
   a) Viruses *87*
   b) Bacteria *89*
   c) Parasites *93*

CHAPTER SEVEN: FEEDING YOUR PEACOCK AND PEAFOWL 97

1) The Basic Peafowl Diet 97
2) Range Feeding 104
3) Supplements 108
4) Feeding Peachicks 110

CHAPTER EIGHT: SOCIALIZING YOUR PEACOCK AND PEAFOWL 112

1) Creating a Friendlier Peafowl 112
2) Keeping your Peafowl at Home 115
3) Peafowl and Pets 118

CHAPTER NINE: NESTING AND BREEDING 120

1)Breeding 121
2) Laying 123
3) Incubation 124
4) Hatching 129
5) Young Peachicks 130

CHAPTER TEN: COMMON TERMS 133

Chapter One: Introduction

Peacocks! Can you raise them in your own home? This question is always asked with surprise and while I don't recommend peacocks and peafowl for an apartment, if you have an adequate yard, the answer is always yes.

The reason why I started with a question is to highlight the uncertainty that has probably brought you to this book. You may be interested in having a peacock but you may not be sure if, or even how, to go about owning one. In one simple paragraph, I have answered at least one of your questions and the rest will be answered throughout this guide.

Although the term peacock is applied to a single bird, there are several terms that anyone interested in raising peafowl should be familiar with. One, peacock identifies the brilliant blue or green birds that we commonly know. Two, peafowl refers to any type of pea species or variety and includes both males and females. Three, peahens are the females in the peafowl species.

The peacock is a beautiful creature and it is one that has captured the hearts and imaginations of people around the world. In fact, the peacock has been revered for millennia and even the Roman goddess Juno was linked to the bird. In her story, her chariot was drawn, not by horses, but by splendid peacocks, their colours flashing and eyes shining.

Today, many people can recall childhood memories of trips to zoos, and in those memories, the peacock, walking gracefully across the green or perching on a fence, is a prominent feature.

I have lost count of the number of peacocks spied roaming around a zoo but for many years, I thought they were simply a bird that can only be found there. I didn't think that I would be able to bring it into my own home to grace my property.

Of course, the first step in any type of journey is always discovering where you want to start and after researching peacocks, I realized that I could bring them into my own home.

In addition, I realized that there was not a lot of information available to fans of the beautiful birds –

information such as what to feed your birds, how to house them properly in all climates and how to ensure that your next generation of peafowl are healthier than your first. All of that information was missing for new enthusiasts to these creatures.

It was that lack of information that influenced me to take my own understanding of peacocks and peafowl and turn it into an informative book that will answer all of your questions. Throughout this book, I have covered how to find the best breeder for your starting birds to how to bring those birds home.

This book covers feeding, daily care, grooming, socializing and finally nesting and breeding your

birds. It is a complete guide and is the only resource that you will need to successfully raise your own peafowl. This book also looks at all of the species of peafowl you can raise.

To say that owning your own peafowl or peacock is a joy is quite an understatement. There is often a sense of wildness to a peacock and the sound of its Yeehaa call, made famous in many movies, is a welcomed addition to any enthusiast's yard.

The brilliant plumage and amazing temperament of these birds will inspire not only your appreciation for their beauty but also an appreciation for their unique characteristics.

Whilst many feel that peacocks are more of an exotic accessory for your home, they are actually a very companionable bird. They enjoy human company and while they are not as attentive as a dog, they will interact with the people who care for them.

In fact, raising peafowl and peacocks can be a very rewarding experience simply because of how amazing and gregarious these birds truly are. They are not an accessory, but a beautiful companion.

The beauty, grace and benefits of owning and raising these birds will be explained throughout this book and it is with those words that I want to help you to take your first step towards owning a peacock.

Chapter Two: Understanding Peacocks and Peafowl

What came first? The peacock or the egg? Okay, maybe the question is about a chicken but when it comes to owning peafowl, it is important to start with the egg first. Yes, you can buy grown birds but in this sense, the egg is key to understanding the bird and where it came from.

The history of the peacock goes back many years and, as I have mentioned in the introduction, the bird can be traced back to ancient Greece and Rome. In addition, it is one of the few animals to be mentioned in the bible and has been revered and cherished by many cultures since antiquity.

In this chapter of the book, I will go over the history of the peacock and will also answer some of the most common questions asked about peacocks.

1) Short History of the Peacock

The peacock has been revered for thousands of years, and although the peacock has been found throughout the world as both domestic pets and feral communities, the peacock is native to India and

Burma. In fact, you can still see several species of peafowl in India and Burma.

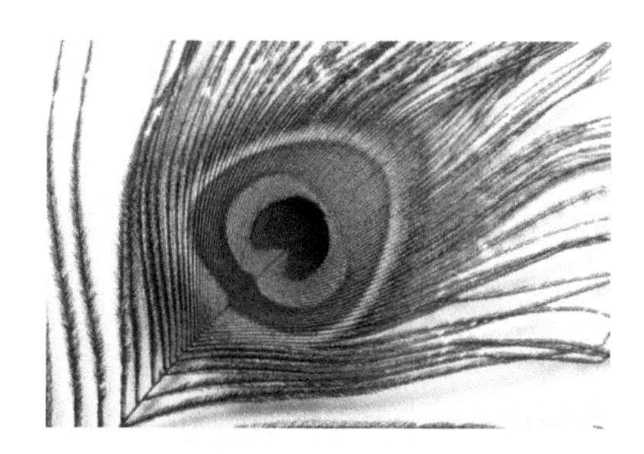

Throughout history, the peacock has been admired for its plumage. It was imported into Egypt and while it is not clear how they were imported, many historians believe that the bird arrived in Egypt with the Phoenicians. From Egypt, peacocks spread throughout the Mediterranean. They have been linked to many ancient gods in several cultures including Ancient Greek, Ancient Romans, and Hinduism.

By the 1300`s, peafowl were found throughout Europe and were a popular sign of wealth and sophistication. Many rich landowners and nobility had peacocks and peafowl on their properties.

This trend continued throughout history and the peacock became a status symbol throughout the world. It was domesticated partly for homes and also for zoos and it has also been adopted as a symbol for modern culture, television stations and religions.

Although the peacock has a long history with its native home, it was not officially accepted as the state bird of India until 1963. It is considered a sacred bird in India and is protected by the Indian law.

In the rest of the world, the peacock and peafowl still make delightful pets that are as graceful as they are beautiful.

2) General Facts about Peafowl

Now that we have gone over the history of peafowl, it

is time to cover some basic facts about the birds. Remember that many of these questions will be answered fully later on in this book, but for right now, I have provided you with some answers to the most pressing questions.

Do peafowl make good pets?

The answer to this question is both a yes and a no and it really depends on what type of pet you are looking for. If you are looking for one that dotes on you, then no, the peacock and peafowl are not for you. However, if you are looking for a charming companion that will alert you to strange things, then yes, they are excellent companions.

Are they good with children?

Generally, peafowl will ignore children but, as with all animals, you should not leave a child unattended with a peacock or peafowl. They may view the child as a threat and can be aggressive during nesting season.

Are they clean?

Although peacocks and peafowl are considered to be fairly clean, they are not recommended for apartments or for inside. They do require their own space like other livestock and will go to the washroom inside if they are brought in.

Can they live in cold climates?

Despite the fact that peacocks are a tropical bird whose natural habitat is a warm climate, they survive surprisingly well in colder climates. In fact, with proper shelter and care, peacocks and peafowl can live in climates that fall below 0 degrees in the winter.

Are they noisy?

The answer to this question is both yes and no. Many times during the year, peafowl are quiet and are a well-mannered bird, however, peacocks tend to become nosier during mating season.

What is the lifespan of a peacock?

If you are looking for a short lived pet, then the peacock is not the proper pet for you. This bird tends to have a very long lifespan, with the bird living 15 to 20 years in the wild and up to 40 years in captivity, on average.

Are there different types of peafowl?

There are several varieties of peafowl and peacocks, but the most common domestic peafowl are the Indian Blue, which have the widespread blue and green colouring that most people are familiar with. There is also the Spalding Peacock, which is a cross between the Indian Blue and the Green Peafowl.

What colours are peacocks?

If you are looking at the colour of a peahen, which is a female peafowl, then you should expect a bird that is brownish in colour with a pale brown mottling over the body. The lower neck is metallic green and the crest on the head is chestnut edged in green. The chest of a peahen is usually a dark brown that is glossed with green and the rest of the belly is white in colour. Despite being a brown bird, they are actually very attractive, however, it is the male peafowl that have the more striking colours that we expect in a peacock.

Peacocks are commonly found in the variety known as the Indian Blue. This is the bird that is metallic blue and green and has very distinct colours. The head itself is metallic blue at the crown and iridescent

greenish blue feathers on the side of the head. There should be white skin under each eye and there should be a fan shaped crest that has black shafts and bluish green webbing on the feathers.

The back of the peacock should be a bronze green with copper and black markings and the tail is dark brown. The tail of a fully grown peacock has long feathers that end in either a crescent black tip or the

elaborate eye spot that is characteristic to the bird. Over 200 feathers make up the elaborate train that the bird can hold up and display.
While the majority of peacocks and peafowl are found in these colour patterns, you can also find white peacocks and pied peacocks. In addition, there are black shouldered peacocks.

In chapter four, I will go over more information, on not only the different types of peacocks, but also the different types of peafowl that you can add to your farm.

How big do peacocks and peahens get?

Although the train can be quite impressive on a peacock, in general, a peacock is usually 40 to 46 inches in length when fully grown, from beak to tail without the train, and they weigh about 8 to 14 pounds on average. The train itself usually grows an additional 78 to 90 inches. Peahens are slightly smaller and are usually 36 to 38 inches in length and weigh 6 to 9 pounds.

Are they difficult to care for?

Like all pets, peacocks and peafowl present their own challenges but if you have the proper housing and set up for the peafowl, then they are not usually difficult to care for.

How long do they take to mature?

Although a peacock or peafowl can reach their full size early, the peahens do not fully mature until 2 years. Peacocks do not mature fully until they are closer to 3 years old. At this time, the peacocks and peafowl can be used in a breeding program.

3) Temperament of Peacocks and Peafowl

Temperament of peacocks and peafowl can differ between species and subspecies; however, since the majority of domestic peafowl are Indian Blues, they generally have the same type of temperament.

When we look at the temperament of peafowl, it is important to look at the males separately from the females.

Generally, peahens are a quiet and gentle bird. They are not usually over excitable and they tend to be very hardy birds. They do have a very innate grace and while they can be aggressive when they or their young are attacked, peahens tend to be very laid back birds.

Peacocks, in turn, show many of the same personalities as the peahens. Usually, they do not have an agitated temperament but they can be quite protective. During mating season, they do become more aggressive and can become quite territorial.

The rest of the year, peacocks become very quiet and gentle birds that simply go about their day to day activities.

It should be stressed that peacocks and peafowl are not domesticated in the true sense of the word. For this reason, you can expect many of the same behaviors of wild peacocks. They will nest and will often try to fly away. In addition, the peafowl will be wary of people approaching them; however, with proper luring and socialization, peafowl will come within a few feet of their owners to eat.

Any potential owner of peafowl should remember that this is not a bird you can carry around or pet.

Despite answering some of the basic questions in this chapter, it is important to look at all the aspects of raising, caring for and breeding your peacocks and peafowl.

Chapter Three: Are you ready to Raise Peacocks and Peafowls

Now that some of your questions about peacocks and peafowl have been answered, it is time to decide if you are ready to raise your own. Remember, that any type of animal you bring into your home is going to take a large commitment from you and peafowl are no exception.

This is a bird that needs space as well as the proper set up in order for them to thrive, so it is important to have both of these before you even consider bringing a peacock home.

Before you purchase a peacock or any type of peafowl, it is important to ask yourself a few questions since peafowl have an exceptionally long life. These are not pets that you purchase for the short term as you can expect at least 20 years with your birds, if not longer.

Do you rent or own?

If you rent a home, then you should avoid purchasing a peafowl, even if you rent a large farm. Unlike dogs and cats, peafowl are not animals that you can move into an apartment if you have to move to a new

rental. Remember that this is a long term animal that needs a good sized backyard space.

What type of dwelling do you live in?

Although peacocks and peafowl can do well in a smaller style of yard, homes with acreage are the better choice for these birds since they do enjoy roaming on their property. In addition, peacocks can be very noisy during mating season and this makes them less ideal for city dwellings. However, they have done well in communities that allow livestock such as chickens in backyards. They are not recommended for apartments and need a yard.

Do you have the time?

Although peafowl are not as time consuming as other pets, you do need to have enough time to care for them properly. Keeping their bedding clean, making sure they stay on your property and feeding them take a daily commitment. If you cannot make that kind of commitment, then you should avoid purchasing your own peafowl.

Are you looking for an affectionate pet?

If the answer is yes, then the peacock is not the right pet for you. This is a semi domesticated animal so they do not usually get too close to their owners. Even ones that have been socialized enough to a handler will still stay a few feet away and will not be a bird that likes to perch on their owner's shoulder or even be near their owner.

Do you have access to an avian vet?

All animals, including peafowl, require regular medical care, so it is important to have an avian vet in your area. If you do not, then it may not be the ideal situation for your peafowl. Vets specializing in birds will understand the many challenges that owning a peacock can have and they will be able to help you maintain the best health for your birds.

Can you provide the proper safety for your pet?

Lastly, providing the proper safety for your peafowl is very important since this bird can often fall victim to foxes and other predators. They will defend their young and nest; however, it is up to the breeder and owner to really make sure that the proper safety measures are in place for their peafowl to prevent them being attacked and or injured.

One thing that should be pointed out is that a peacock cannot be made to fit into a lifestyle. These are birds that require space and proper care and you need to be willing and able to provide both.

1) Pros and Cons of Owning Peafowl

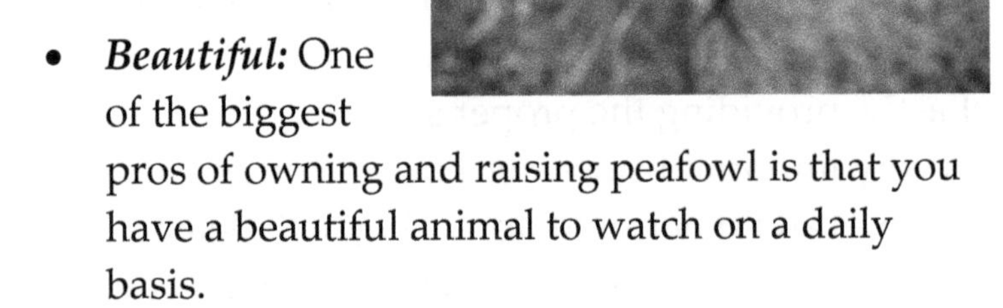

Like every other type of animal, there are a number of pros and cons that you should consider before you purchase your own birds and I will go over both of them to help you make the best decision.

Pros of Owning a Peafowl

- ***Beautiful:*** One of the biggest pros of owning and raising peafowl is that you have a beautiful animal to watch on a daily basis.

- ***Quiet:*** Generally, peafowl are quiet birds. There are periods of the season when they aren't but for most of the year you shouldn't have too much noise.

- ***Easy Care:*** Peafowl are very easy to care for and have many of the same needs that chickens have. Vaccinations are necessary, as is proper housing but they don't require a lot of extra care.

- ***Profitable:*** If you are interested in breeding peafowl, you can actually make a fair amount of profit if you do it properly.

- ***Guarding:*** No, they generally won't attack an intruder; however, most peafowl will make noise if something is unusual in the yard.

- ***Inexpensive:*** While you can pay a large amount for some types of peafowl, the actual cost of care is quite low. Many do very well on inexpensive feeds and outside of the start up costs and vaccination costs; you won't have a large amount of upkeep costs.

Generally, peafowl are an easy bird to raise and care for and the biggest advantage of owning a peafowl is simply the joy of watching the inquisitive birds in the yard.

Cons of Owning a Peafowl

- ***Noise:*** While peafowl are fairly quiet during most of the year, during the breeding season, both peahens and peacocks can be quite noisy.

- ***Ranging:*** If you are interested in having your peafowl range through your yard, you should be aware of the fact that they range quite far. In fact, they will often go miles away from home and this can put them at risk of predators or being injured on the highways.

- ***Expensive Start Up:*** Like most animals, the start up can be quite expensive when you take into account the different equipment you need, which I will go over later on in this book.

- ***Predation:*** As I have mentioned, predation can be a problem with peafowl so you will need to be aware of this and also understand how to prevent it.

- ***Dietary Needs:*** While peafowl are usually very easy to care for, dealing with their diet can be a bit overwhelming and can be costly if it is not done properly. Make sure you are aware of this before you purchase your peafowl.

- ***Lifespan:*** The long lifespan of peafowl can be both a bonus and an impulse purchase.

As with all animals, it is important to understand both the challenges and advantages of owning and raising peafowl. Owning them can be wonderful but it is a commitment and shouldn't be a entered into lightly.

2) Free Range or Penned

The last thing that you should consider before you even go to purchase your peafowl is whether you would like to have them free range or whether you want to pen them.

Although it may seem like a simple choice, it isn't. Free ranging peafowl can be wonderful but they can also be very challenging. In addition, penned peafowl can be challenging as well.

What is Free Ranging?

Free ranging your peafowl is when you are able to have the peafowl move around your property without being hindered by pens or fences. Generally, free ranging peafowl become wilder than your penned peafowl and they often forage for themselves, which can cut down on the amount of work involved with feeding them.

What are the Benefits of Free Ranging?

Pros for free ranging your birds can include:

- ***Easier Care:*** Since they are free ranging and taking care of themselves, it can be quite easy to care for the birds. In addition, you don't have to clean out any pens when your birds free range.

- ***Less Cost:*** Generally, the cost of caring for a free range peafowl is less, especially when you look at feeding as the peafowl finds much of its own food

- ***Less Time:*** Ranging peafowl require less of your time and you can simply set up one area for feeding and watering your birds. They will take care of the rest.

- ***Less Space:*** When you first bring your birds home, you will need to have space for your aviary, which I will go over later in this book, but afterwards, the birds don't need a very large set space. This can save time, money and space in your yard.

- ***Amazing to watch:*** Let's face it, the main reason that people purchase peafowl is for the beautiful train of the peacock. Having the birds free range will give you more opportunity to see it and will also give you the chance to watch the birds explore and interact with the world around them.

As you can see, there are many benefits to having your birds free range and it really depends on what you want.

What are the Disadvantages of Free Ranging?

Cons for free ranging your birds can include:

- ***Can disappear:*** Free range peafowl can disappear from your property, especially when

  they are first released. Although people don't realize it, peafowl can fly quite well and can also hop upwards over 30 feet. They will easily jump a 6 foot fence and disappear.

- ***Destructive:*** Free ranging peafowl can be very destructive to a yard and they will eat plants and many other items in your garden if they are allowed to range.

- ***High Predation Rate:*** Although penned peafowl can fall prey to predators, those that free range are at a higher risk from predators. Most predation occurs when the peahens are nesting or have chicks.

- ***High Risk of Injury:*** Since peafowl will range quite far when they are out, they can be more susceptible to injury from roads, people and from eating things that can be harmful to them. This can result in higher vet costs for you or even in the loss or your peafowl.

- ***Indiscriminate Breeding:*** Lastly, when peafowl free range, it can be harder to make your own breeding program to ensure that you get exactly what you want from a pairing.

In the end, the main difference between free ranging and penning your birds is simply the risks involved for your birds. The more they range, the harder it can be to keep them safe, however, having them in the pen can mean it is more difficult to enjoy them to their fullest.

Chapter Four: Choosing the Right Peacock and Peafowl

If you find that you are ready for a peafowl or a peacock, it is now time to start looking for the peafowl that you want to have. Although you may not be aware of it, there are over 180 different varieties of peafowl and it can make choosing the right one quite difficult.

In this chapter, I will cover aspects of choosing the right type of peafowl as well as what to look for in your peafowl breeder and how to sex your birds.

1) Types of Peafowl

Although we often think of peacocks when we think of peafowl, there are actually many different varieties and it is important to be aware of them. Most peafowl are raised in the same manner; however, there are some slight differences in some of them.

Peafowl come in several different types with a number of varieties in each subspecies.

a) Species

There are two species of peafowl, which are known as the Pavo Cristatus and the Pavo Muticus and one hybrid species of peafowl, known as the Spalding.

Pavo Cristatus:

Also known as the Indian Blue Peafowl, Blue Peafowl or India Peafowl, this is the more common of the peacock species.

While there are patterns in the Indian Blue Peafowl, the main snapshot of the bird is as follows:

Indian Blue

As I have mentioned many times, Indian Blues are the more common peacock found in zoos and on farms. These are the birds that are usually depicted in art.

Ease of Raising: Very Easy, good for new breeders
Origin: India, Burma and Malaya
Coloration:

- ***Peacock:*** Blue chest, neck and head with white and black striped shoulders and hints of green and gold feathers throughout the bird. The long tail has a large eye or crescent pattern.
- ***Peahen:*** Brown in colour, the Indian Blue peahen also have iridescent green on their neck as well as a white belly.
- ***Peachick:*** Greyish-brown in colour.

Pavo Muticus:

Also known as the Green Peafowl, and there are three subspecies of green peafowl. Green peafowl are not as common as Indian Blue Peafowl, but they are slowly gaining some popularity with breeders. Green peafowl tend to be slightly taller and leaner than blue peafowl. The subspecies of green peafowl are:

Burmese Green

Some varieties of peafowl have been created through cross breeding; however, the Burmese Green is a wild peafowl. They are actually quite rare in captivity and even rarer in the wild. They are an endangered species and while they look similar to an Indian Blue, they have a muted colouring.

Ease of Raising: Medium

Origin: Burma
Coloration:

- ***Peacock:*** Dull blue and green in colour with a dark blue throat and blue back. Wing coverts are black.
- ***Peahen:*** Blue coloration with muted brown and black feathers over their entire body.
- ***Peachick:*** Greyish-brown in colour.

Indo-Chinese Green

Another subspecies of the green peafowl, the Indo Chinese Green are a brilliant green bird that is found in both the wild and in captivity. They are a very rare peafowl to have and only a handful of breeders carry this species.

Ease of Raising: Medium
Origin: Indochina, Eastern Burma and Siam
Coloration:

- ***Peacock:*** Light blue and yellow skin on the face, the body is bluish green with a dark green underside. The neck and head are metallic green. Very similar in colour to the Java Green, however, they are slightly muted in colour.
- ***Peahen:*** Similar coloration to the male Java Green, and can often be mistaken for the other green peafowl. They have muted colours and

the Indo Chinese Green has a buff border around the breast.

- ***Peachick:*** Dark greyish-brown in colour.

Java Green

Also known as the Javanese peafowl, the Java Green is another green peafowl that can be found in the wild as well as in captivity. Again, this bird is endangered; however, they are the most common green peafowl in captivity.

Ease of Raising: Medium
Origin: Java and Malay Peninsula
Coloration:

- ***Peacock:*** Light blue and yellow skin on the face, the body is bluish green with a dark green underside. The neck and head are metallic green.
- ***Peahen:*** Similar coloration to the male Java Green, the peahen has muted colours and dark barring on the tail.
- ***Peachick:*** Dark greyish-brown in colour.

Spalding:

The Spalding was developed by crossing the Green Peafowl with the Indian Blue Peafowl. They are usually lighter than other peafowl and are quickly gaining popularity. The snapshot of the Spalding is:

Ease of Raising: Easy
Origin: California, United States.
Coloration:

- ***Peacock:*** Bluish Green chest, neck and head with white and black striped shoulders and hints of green and gold feathers throughout the bird. There is usually a patch of yellow on the head and the crest is usually shorter than either the Indian Blue or the Green Peafowl. The long tail has a large eye or crescent pattern.
- ***Peahen:*** Similar coloration to other peahens, there is a greenish blue feathering on the neck and chest with a small yellow patch on the face.
- ***Peachick:*** Dark greyish-brown in colour.

b) Patterns

Generally, when you are looking at the different varieties of peafowl that you can choose from, you are actually looking at the patterns of the feathers. There are many different feather patterns; however, they are grouped into the following categories:

Pied

Pied is found in many of the peafowl species and is a colour mutation where the feathers are splotched with white. The mutation is caused by an incomplete dominant gene and you can breed pied from pied birds or by crossing other patterns, although they do not breed true.

Generally, the white can take up a small amount of the feathers or it can take upwards of 60% of the bird. Even the train can have splotches and patches of white. A common snapshot of the pied colouring can be seen in the Indian Blue Pied:

Indian Blue Pied

A pied peafowl is an interesting bird, as it has the colouring of an Indian Blue but will be splotched with white. The pied pattern occurs due to an incomplete dominant gene and it is important to note that the chicks are not always pied. In fact, 25% of the offspring can be born white.

Ease of Raising: Easy
Origin: India
Coloration:

- ***Peacock:*** Blue chest, neck and head with white and completely black shoulders and hints of green and gold feathers throughout the bird. The long tail has a large eye or crescent pattern. The entire bird is covered with splotches and patches of white and some have white on their train.
- ***Peahen:*** Brown in colour, the peahen also has iridescent green on their neck as well as a white belly. Again, the peahen can be covered in white splotches.
- ***Peachick:*** Light yellow with brown wings.

Other types of pied patterning are:

- Black Shoulder Pied
- Black Shoulder Pied White-Eyed
- Cameo Black Shoulder Pied
- Cameo Black Shoulder Pied White-Eyed
- Cameo Pied White
- Indian Blue Pied
- India Blue Pied White-Eyed
- Charcoal Pied
- Charcoal Pied White-Eyed

- Charcoal Black Shoulder Pied
- Charcoal Black Shoulder Pied White-Eyed
- Purple Pied
- Purple Pied White-Eyed
- Purple Black Shoulder Pied
- Purple Black Shoulder Pied White-Eyed
- Buford Bronze Pied
- Buford Bronze Pied White-Eyed
- Buford Bronze Black Shoulder Pied
- Buford Bronze Black Shoulder Pied White-Eyed
- Peach Pied
- Peach Pied White-Eyed
- Peach Black Shoulder Pied
- Peach Black Shoulder Pied White-Eyed
- Opal Pied
- Opal Pied White-Eyed
- Opal Black Shoulder Pied White-Eyed
- Opal Black Shoulder Pied
- Midnight Pied
- Midnight Pied White-Eyed
- Midnight Black Shoulder Pied White-Eyed
- Jade Pied
- Midnight Black Shoulder Pied
- Jade Pied White-Eyed
- Jade Black Shoulder Pied
- Jade Black Shoulder Pied White-Eyed
- Taupe Pied
- Taupe Pied White-Eyed
- Taupe Black Shoulder Pied

- Taupe Black Shoulder Pied White-Eyed
- Sonja's Violete Pied White-Eyed
- Sonja's Violete Silver Pied
- Sonja's Violete Black Shoulder Pied
- Sonja's Violete Black Shoulder Pied White-Eyed
- Sonja's Violete Pied
- Spalding Pied
- Spalding Pied White-Eyed
- Spalding Black Shoulder Pied
- Spalding Black Shoulder Pied White-Eyed
- Spalding Cameo Pied
- Spalding Cameo Pied White-Eyed
- Spalding Cameo Black Shoulder Pied White-Eyed
- Spalding Cameo Black Shoulder Pied
- Spalding Charcoal Pied
- Spalding Charcoal Pied White-Eyed
- Spalding Charcoal Black Shoulder Pied
- Spalding Charcoal Black Shoulder Pied White-Eyed
- Spalding Purple Pied
- Spalding Purple Pied White-Eyed
- Spalding Purple Black Shoulder Pied
- Spalding Purple Black Shoulder Pied White-Eyed
- Spalding Buford Bronze Pied
- Spalding Buford Bronze Pied White-Eyed
- Spalding Buford Bronze Black Shoulder Pied White-Eyed

- Spalding Buford Bronze Black Shoulder Pied
- Spalding Peach Pied
- Spalding Peach Pied White-Eyed
- Spalding Peach Black Shoulder Pied
- Spalding Peach Black Shoulder Pied White-Eyed
- Spalding Opal Pied
- Spalding Opal Pied White-Eyed
- Spalding Opal Black Shoulder Pied
- Spalding Opal Black Shoulder Pied White-Eyed
- Spalding Midnight Pied
- Spalding Midnight Pied White-Eyed
- Spalding Midnight Black Shoulder Pied
- Spalding Midnight Black Shoulder Pied White-Eyed
- Spalding Jade Pied
- Spalding Jade Pied White-Eyed
- Spalding Jade Black Shoulder Pied
- Spalding Jade Black Shoulder Pied White-Eyed
- Spalding Taupe Pied
- Spalding Taupe Pied White-Eyed
- Spalding Taupe Black Shoulder Pied
- Spalding Taupe Black Shoulder Pied White-Eyed
- Spalding Sonja's Violete Pied
- Spalding Sonja's Violete Pied White-Eyed
- Spalding Sonja's Violete Black Shoulder Pied
- Spalding Sonja's Violete Black Shoulder Pied White-Eyed

Silver Pied:

Although this is a similar colour mutation as you would see with the pied, the silver pied is when the feathers have a slightly silvery colouring to them.

The silver pied is seen in the Indian Blue peafowl and while they will produce silver pied offspring, they will also produce white eyed and pure white offspring. The snapshot of a silver pied is:

Ease of Raising: Medium, if you are trying to produce Silver Pied only in your hatchlings, then it can be a bit difficult.
Origin: India
Coloration:

- ***Peacock:*** Predominantly white with about 10 to 20 percent of the body and head collared with blue or green feathers. The ocelli in the train should have a white centre.
- ***Peahen:*** Predominantly white with a few patches of grey. Although it is not present all of the time, many peahens will have a patch of green on the neck.
- ***Peachick:*** Yellowish white, the chick will also have some brown specks on the head and a brown spot on the back.

Other types of Black Shoulder patterning are:

- Black Shoulder Silver Pied
- Buford Bronze Silver Pied
- Cameo Black Shoulder Silver Pied
- Cameo Silver Pied
- India Blue Silver Pied
- Charcoal Silver Pied
- Charcoal Black Shoulder Silver Pied
- Purple Silver Pied
- Purple Black Shoulder Silver Pied
- Buford Bronze Black Shoulder Silver Pied
- Peach Silver Pied
- Peach Black Shoulder Silver Pied
- Opal Silver Pied
- Opal Black Shoulder Silver Pied
- Midnight Silver Pied
- Midnight Black Shoulder Silver Pied
- Jade Silver Pied
- Jade Black Shoulder Silver Pied

- Taupe Silver Pied

- Taupe Black Shoulder Silver Pied
- Sonja's Violete Black Shoulder Silver Pied
- Spalding Silver Pied

- Spalding Cameo Silver Pied
- Spalding Black Shoulder Silver Pied
- Spalding Cameo Black Shoulder Silver Pied
- Spalding Charcoal Silver Pied
- Spalding Charcoal Black Shoulder Silver Pied
- Spalding Purple Silver Pied
- Spalding Purple Black Shoulder Silver Pied
- Spalding Buford Bronze Silver Pied
- Spalding Buford Bronze Black Shoulder Silver Pied
- Spalding Peach Silver Pied
- Spalding Peach Black Shoulder Silver Pied
- Spalding Opal Silver Pied
- Spalding Opal Black Shoulder Silver Pied
- Spalding Midnight Silver Pied
- Spalding Midnight Black Shoulder Silver Pied
- Spalding Jade Silver Pied
- Spalding Jade Black Shoulder Silver Pied
- Spalding Taupe Silver Pied
- Spalding Taupe Black Shoulder Silver Pied

- Spalding Sonja's Violete Silver Pied
- Spalding Sonja's Violete Black Shoulder Silver Pied

Black Shoulder:

Another colour mutation, the black shoulder birds are peafowl that have dark black shoulders instead of the bars seen in other birds.

The main species that the black shoulder comes from is the Indian Blue, although you can find them in a variety of colours, which are listed below.

The Black Shoulder is one of the most common peafowl that is seen in captivity and it was first discovered in 1823 in India. The snapshot of a Black Shoulder is:

Ease of Raising: Easy
Origin: India and America
Coloration:

- ***Peacock:*** Blue chest, neck and head with white and completely black shoulders and hints of green and gold feathers throughout the bird. The long tail has a large eye or crescent pattern.
- ***Peahen:*** A white bird with black splotches, the peahen also has a reddish-tan patch of feathers on her neck.
- ***Peachick:*** Light yellow with peach collared wings.

Other types of Black Shoulder patterning are:

- Black Shoulder
- Cameo Black Shoulder
- Cameo Black Shoulder White-Eyed
- Charcoal Black Shoulder
- Charcoal Black Shoulder White-Eyed
- Purple Black Shoulder
- Purple Black Shoulder White-Eyed
- Buford Bronze Black Shoulder
- Buford Bronze Black Shoulder White-Eyed
- Peach Black Shoulder

- Peach Black Shoulder White-Eyed
- Opal Black Shoulder
- Opal Black Shoulder White-Eyed
- Midnight Black Shoulder
- Midnight Black Shoulder White-Eyed
- Jade Black Shoulder
- Jade Black Shoulder White-Eyed
- Taupe Black Shoulder
- Taupe Black Shoulder White-Eyed
- Sonja's Violete Black Shoulder
- Sonja's Violete Black Shoulder White-Eyed
- Spalding Black Shoulder
- Spalding Black Shoulder White-Eyed
- Spalding Cameo Black Shoulder
- Spalding Cameo Black Shoulder White-Eyed
- Spalding Charcoal Black Shoulder
- Spalding Charcoal Black Shoulder White-Eyed
- Spalding Purple Black Shoulder
- Spalding Purple Black Shoulder White-Eyed
- Spalding Buford Bronze Black Shoulder
- Spalding Buford Bronze Black Shoulder White-Eyed
- Spalding Peach Black Shoulder
- Spalding Peach Black Shoulder White-Eyed
- Spalding Opal Black Shoulder
- Spalding Opal Black Shoulder White-Eyed

- Spalding Midnight Black Shoulder
- Spalding Midnight Black Shoulder White-Eyed
- Spalding Jade Black Shoulder
- Spalding Jade Black Shoulder White-Eyed
- Spalding Taupe Black Shoulder
- Spalding Taupe Black Shoulder White-Eyed
- Spalding Sonja's Violete Black Shoulder
- Spalding Sonja's Violete Black Shoulder White-Eyed

White-Eyed

The white eyed peacock has a very interesting pattern as it is actually seen in the train and not in the overall feather patterning of the birds. It is when you see a small dot of white in the centre each of the ocelli, or eyespot, on the bird's train. The amount of colour can vary from bird to bird. Below is a snapshot of the white eye.

Ease of Raising: Medium, they will produce white eyed at a high rate depending on what they are bred with.
Origin: India
Coloration:

- ***Peacock:*** Blue chest, neck and head with white and completely black shoulders and hints of green and gold feathers throughout the bird. There should also be a patch of white on the throat and the ocelli on the train should have a white centre.

- ***Peahen:*** Brown in colour, the peahen also has a white belly. In addition, there should be a white patch on the throat and there should be silver tipping of the feathers.
- ***Peachick:*** Light yellow with brown wings

Other varieties of white-eye patterning are:

- India Blue White-Eyed
- Black Shoulder White-Eyed
- Cameo White-Eyed
- Charcoal White-Eyed
- Purple White-Eyed
- Buford Bronze White-Eyed
- Peach White-Eyed
- Opal White-Eyed
- Midnight White-Eyed
- Jade White-Eyed
- Taupe White-Eyed
- Sonja's Violete White-Eyed
- Spalding White-Eyed
- Spalding Cameo White-Eyed
- Spalding Charcoal White-Eyed
- Spalding Buford Bronze White-Eyed
- Spalding Opal White-Eyed
- Spalding Midnight White-Eyed

- Spalding Jade White-Eyed
- Spalding Taupe White-Eyed
- Spalding Sonja's Violete White-Eyed

c) Colours

In addition to patterns, there are a few colour variations that you can find in the peafowl and they are commonly found in both the Indian Blue and the hybrid species Spalding. Although all of the colours can have white eye, black shoulder, pied and silver pied, it is important to understand how a peafowl will look with the different colour variations.

Cameo

A colour mutation that is seen in Indian Blues, you can also find the colour mutation in Spaldings. The colour itself was the first colour mutation to be discovered. It originated in Maine, United States and was developed in the 1960's.

It is one of the more common colour mutations, placing second only to white. An interesting fact about the Cameo is that it is a sex linked mutation. Males pass the gene onto the young so if a Cameo male is bred to any other colour, all of the female chicks will be Cameos while the males will be a split between Cameo, Indian Blue and whatever colour the hen was. Cameo females will not produce Cameos unless they are bred to another Cameo.

The snapshot of the Cameo is:

Ease of Raising: Medium
Origin: Maine, United States by an Oscar Mulloy. Sherman Cram, Dennis Cook, and Norman Waycott
Coloration:

- ***Peacock:*** A dark brown that softens to a coffee milk colour during moulting. The neck is a darker shade of brown and the train is a dark brown with varying shades of brown in the eyespot. There is no iridescent colouring on the cameo.
- ***Peahen:*** Peahens are a light, creamy brown in colour and should be lighter than males. They should have a lighter chest and back but they should also have dark rust on the head and neck.
- ***Peachick:*** Light creamy brown in colour.

White

The white peafowl is actually a subspecies of the Indian

Blue and is caused by a mutation in the genes that result in a white colour. It is important to note that these peafowl are not albinos and are simply white.

Ease of Raising: Medium-Hard: One of the main problems is an inability to determine their gender before 2 years of age.
Origin: India
Coloration:

- ***Peacock:*** Completely white with a small eyespot of off white on their train.
- ***Peahen:*** Peahens are completely white and have vibrant blue eyes.
- ***Peachick:*** Yellow in colouring with white wings.

Purple

One of the rarest colours that you can find, purple is actually a fairly new colour mutation. It has been seen as early as 1987; however, the purple was not fully accepted until 1994.

Like the Cameo colour, purple is a colour mutation that is sex linked. Peacocks pass the colour to their offspring, and any male that is bred to a non-purple female won't produce as many male purple peacocks as he does hens. The result is that there are fewer male purples available.

One interesting point about purple peafowl is that their colour often becomes quite muted in the summer month and almost looks like a Cameo.

A snapshot of the purple is:

Ease of Raising: Medium
Origin: Arizona, United States by Jack Siepel and later developed by Roughwood Aviaries
Coloration:

- ***Peacock:*** Very similar to the Indian Blue, the peacock has shades of purple on the chest, head and neck. It also has white and black striped shoulders and hints of purple and gold feathers throughout the bird. The long tail has a large eye or crescent pattern and is purple and green near the ocelli. As the bird ages, the train becomes cameo in colour with the brightly coloured ocelli.
- ***Peahen:*** Peahens are a light, creamy brown in colour. They should have a lighter chest and back but they should also have dark rust on the head and neck. They usually have a purple patch on their neck.
- ***Peachick:*** Light creamy brown in colour.

Buford Bronze

The Buford Bronze is a brown peafowl that is one of the rare colours of peafowl. It was first developed in the 1980's and while they are a beautiful bird, they are not as widely known as other colour variations.

Ease of Raising: Easy
Origin: United States by Buford Abbolt
Coloration:

- ***Peacock:*** A chocolate brown bird, the peacock is a very dark brown with a train that features dark brown ocelli. There is usually a slight iridescence on the train.
- ***Peahen:*** Peahens are a light, creamy brown in colour. They should have a lighter chest and back but they should also have dark brown on the head and neck.
- ***Peachick:*** Light creamy brown in colour.

Opal

The opal peafowl is another colour mutation that is still quite new. In fact, the colour was first recognized in 2001 and the birds are still very hard to come by. The name was given to the birds due to the hints of aquamarine in the feathers that give a jewelled effect.

Ease of Raising: Easy
Origin: United States by David Dickerson of Delaware and Dwayne Jones of Maryland in the 1990's.
Coloration:

- ***Peacock:*** A brown bird with a dark brown head and neck that also has hints of aquamarine in the feathers. The shoulders are barred with two shades of brown and the train has ocelli that are black, copper and opal.
- ***Peahen:*** A light grey bird with a slightly darker grey patch on the neck.
- ***Peachick:*** A whitish-grey bird.

Charcoal

Another rare colour, charcoal, was originally developed in the 1980's but due to an unfortunate trait; the colour variation has remained fairly unknown.

The main problem with the trait is that many charcoals do not lay fertile eggs and this has kept the numbers down and made them quite difficult to raise and breed.

Ease of Raising: Difficult
Origin: Arizona, United States by the Phoenix Zoo.
Coloration:

- ***Peacock:*** A black bird that has a dark, greyish black train with eyespots that are varying shades of black. The colour is very dull and there is no iridescence.
- ***Peahen:*** A dark grey bird with a charcoal neck and an off white breast.

- ***Peachick:*** Greyish-brown in colour.

Peach

Peach is another sex linked colour, where the colour is passed down from the males and can only be produced by the hens if they are bred to another peach. The colour is quite new and very rare and it may be difficult and expensive to purchase your own peach peafowl.

Ease of Raising: Medium
Origin: United States
Coloration:

- ***Peacock:*** The feathers are a light orangey, brown colour with a train that has similar shades as the rest of the coat. The tail and the wings usually fade to an off-white colour as they mature.

- ***Peahen:*** Peahens are a very light, creamy orangey-brown in colour. They should have a lighter chest and back but they should also have a darker shade on the head and neck. They look very similar to the Cameo peahen, only lighter
- ***Peachick:*** Light creamy brown in colour with an orange tint.

Midnight

The final colour that is recognized in peafowl is the midnight colour. This is a blue bird that looks very similar to the Indian Blue; however, the colouring is a much darker blue. It is still a very rare colour, which makes it quite expensive and has only been around since 1998.

Ease of Raising: Easy
Origin: United States
Coloration:

- ***Peacock:*** Blue chest, neck and head with white and black striped shoulders and hints of green and gold feathers throughout the bird. The long tail has a large eye or crescent pattern. The blue on the bird is a very dark, almost midnight, blue.

- ***Peahen:*** Brown in colour, the Indian Blue peahen also have iridescent green on their neck as well as a white belly.
- ***Peachick:*** Greyish-brown in colour.

2) Choosing Your Peafowl

At this point, you may realize that there are a lot of different peafowl and it can be a bit overwhelming when you are trying to decide on your own peafowl.

Although everyone has a favourite peafowl, I always recommend that new enthusiasts take the time to research each of the varieties. The main point that you should look at is what type of colour you are interested in before you actually start narrowing down the birds you want to bring in.

The first place that I recommend you start is to go through the UPA, United Peacock Association at http://www.peafowl.org. This organization not only has peafowl for sale, but it can direct you to breeders of many different colour and pattern variations. They can also answer questions that you have specific to the peacock species and is an excellent resource to have.

When you have narrowed it down to a colour or species that you want, then it is time to decide between adults and chicks.

Generally, I recommend that all new enthusiasts start with adults, although you can start with young adults. Chicks can be a bit more difficult to raise, since they need some special diets; such as starter feeds and they do require the care and protection of their mother peahen.

Some of the benefits of starting with a chick are:

- ***Can socialize them your own way:*** While they will never be completely tame, some breeders have found that handling chicks when they are young can encourage a stronger bond between bird and owner.

- ***Enjoyment:*** Watching the peafowl grow can be just as entertaining and delightful as watching the full grown peafowl.

- ***Less Noise:*** Because peafowl do not reach maturity until they are roughly 2 years of age, there is a longer period of time without any loud noises.

Cons of purchasing chicks are:

- ***More work:*** Chicks require a bit more care than an adult peafowl and you will need a better set up so the chicks stay warm.

- ***Difficult to Sex:*** Some peafowl can be sexed, where you determine the gender, very easily while others can be very difficult. In some cases, such as whites, it can take over 2 years to determine if the peafowl is male or female.

- ***Longer Wait:*** Most males do not begin to have a train until they are over 2 years of age and some may not have a full train until they are 5 years of age. Starting with a chick means that it will be that much longer before you can enjoy the beauty of the peacock.

With adult peafowl, you will have to make do with the temperament that the breeder established. If the birds were left on their own a lot, you may find that they are a bit more skittish with humans than ones that have been socialized.

When you are choosing peafowl, take your time choosing your breeder. Here are a few points with the breeder that you should consider:

1. ***How long has the breeder been raising peafowl?*** Although you can go with a newly established breeder, it is better to go with one that has been established for a long time. These breeders often become a resource for you and will help you set up your space.

2. ***Is the breeder open to discuss peafowl?*** If the breeder is just trying to sell you the peafowl, then you should probably look elsewhere. As I have already mentioned, you really want a peafowl breeder who will answer the questions you have.

3. ***Is the facility clean?*** It may be more difficult to gauge the facility if the peafowl are free to roam, but you should make sure that the nesting areas are clean and that there isn't a lot of filth where the birds are. In addition, make sure that there is no overcrowding in any pens that are set up.

4. ***Are the birds healthy?*** Make sure that all the birds you see are healthy. Ask about their worming schedule, when the last time the birds were wormed and what they do to oversee the health of the birds. If you find that the birds look underweight or their feathers are dull, then you should look elsewhere for your bird.

5. ***Is the breeder part of the NPIP?*** NPIP means the National Poultry Improvement Program and it is designed to prevent diseases and the spread of diseases in birds, namely poultry. Breeders who are NPIP approved work hard to ensure that the birds they are breeding and raising are free of disease. Starting with an NPIP approved bird will help ensure that your peafowls are healthy.

Although you can purchase only one peafowl, it is often better for both the bird and you to purchase a breeding pair, or male and female. This ensures that you have the ability to produce your own young and you will have double the enjoyment with your birds.

One thing that you should always check is the overall health of your birds. Make sure that the birds have the majority of their feathers, unless it is moulting season, and also make sure that the colouring is right. If you have a bird that is known for having iridescence on the feathers, you will want to make sure that the feathers are iridescent.

In addition, look for birds that have an alert and curious look to them. The neck should be long and strong and a healthy peafowl will hold its head up. Eyes should be clear of any lumps or discoloration and the bird should have an alert look in the eye.

Plumage should be full and the overall shape of the bird should be strong and thick. Overall, the breast should be very thick. Although most people don't look for it, toes should be straight and it is important to make sure that the beak is straight as well.

When you are looking for peafowl, the best rule of thumb is to really go with your gut instinct. If something seems off, then find a different breeder and remember that you do not have to go with the first breeder you find.

Chapter Five: Bringing Your Birds Home

Well, you have done it. You have chosen your bird and you are getting ready to bring it home. Before you do, however, there are a number of things that you should do, such as setting up pens. Bringing your peafowl home properly will ensure that your peafowl have a long and happy life.

1) Special Permits

In general, peafowl do not need any type of special permits to be owned. They are often classified as poultry so they only require the proper zoning laws appropriate to poultry.

One thing that I should mention, is that in most places, there are no special permits needed. However, as they fall under the category of agriculture animals, you need to make sure that you are allowed them in your area.

Some cities and towns allow backyard poultry but others don't. Take the time before you purchase a peafowl to make sure that you are allowed to have them in your area.

In addition to that research, most areas require you to have a clean bill of health on the birds you bring in. This keeps them from spreading diseases into the area, so a transport certificate will need to be cleared with both the Ministry of Agriculture and a local vet.

Once the birds are at your home, you should keep them in quarantine for the time that you are conditioning them to your property to ensure that there is no underlying illness that was overlooked.

2) Pens and Housing

Before you bring your peafowl home, it is important to set up your equipment and housing. Although you may be planning on conditioning your birds (see chapter eight), you will need to have pens to keep the birds safe during the night.

The number of pens can vary, depending on the number of birds that you get, but in general, I recommend that you keep only two birds in each pen so that you don't have a lot of overcrowding.

When you are making a pen, you should consider a few factors. First, you will need an enclosed space where the birds can get out of the cold. You can either make a door for the birds to go in and out of, or you can just make a sheltered section in an outdoor enclosure.

No matter what you choose, I recommend that you build a laneway from all of your pens. The laneway should have a fully enclosed roof, either with wire or in a building, and should be about 8 feet wide and run past all the doors of each pen you have.

The doors of the pens should open fully into the laneway and there should be a door at the end of the laneway for you to access or to send the birds out of. The main reason for this laneway is so that you have added security if a bird runs out of a pen when you enter it.

In addition, it makes sorting much easier and you can simply herd the bird out of a pen and into a different pen. This reduces the amount of stress the birds feel as you will not have to capture the birds.

The pens themselves should consist of an inside stall, usually kept in a barn and the outdoor flight pen. The inside stall should be about 8 feet wide by 8 feet deep. The height should be also about 8 feet and there should be a wooden or wire roof to prevent the birds from flying up.

From the stall, there should be a small door for the birds to access the flight pen. The flight pens should also be 8 feet wide and 8 feet high but the length should be 42 feet long. This may seem like a huge space but, trust me, the birds will be much happier because of it.

Try to place flight pens on the south facing wall as this usually provides them with more depth. Cover the first 10 feet of the flight pen with wood or metal to provide the birds with shade and shelter from rain.

The remaining part of the flight pen should be wire and you should never leave them uncovered. An 8 foot fence is nothing to a peafowl and they can easily jump them.

The wire I recommend that you use for the pens should be a 1 x 2 inch wire and if you can, I recommend that you place 1 inch knotted mesh over the tops of the flight pen as the birds have been known to break through the covers.

When it comes to the environment in the pen, try to grow grass in the majority of the flight pen. If you are unable to, keep the dirt clean and free of debris;

especially man made debris as peafowl will swallow it.
Next, keep a dirt area under the covered portion of the flight pen and also add a small amount of hay or straw. In the stall, cover the floor with hay or straw.

3) Building a Roost

In the pen and stall, make sure you have an area for the birds to roost. Roosts should be installed about 4 feet off of the ground, so the bird can easily get up without hitting the ceiling of the pen.

Roosts can be both heated or non-heated but generally, you should avoid using heated if you live in warm climates. If you live in a cold climate, then a few heated roosts can help keep temperatures bearable for the birds.

A heated roost is very easy to make. Run a strip of electric heat tape, which is used on water pipes, down the length of a 2 x 6 board twice. You want to leave 6 inches on either side of the roost.

Next, secure the tape with staples and hang the thermostat in a way so you can read the temperature easily.

Wrap the roost with thick carpet and leave a 4 inch space on either end of the board that is not lined with carpet.

Install the roost in the pen and if you need to, reinforce it with a second board to keep it from bowing.

4) Protection from Predators

If your peafowl are free ranging, there is not a lot that you can do to protect them from predators. I recommend that you keep them in an enclosure during the night but if you can't, then you should allow the trees in your yard to have branches of about 10 feet above the ground.

Thin out the trees a bit for better roosting but not too much, as the birds will not feel protected. Have enough roosting spots in your yard so the birds can see the space around them clearly.

For birds that are in a pen, constantly check the pen to make sure that the wire has not been disturbed. In addition, bury the 1 x 2 inch wire underground about 2 feet to prevent burrowing predators from getting at your birds.

For ones that will try to climb up and chew into the pen, you can place an electric fence part way up the pen. This will deter any larger predators as well.

5) Bringing the Peafowl Home

Now that you have your pen and roosting set up for your peafowl, it is time to bring the peafowl home. One point that I should mention is that you should purchase your peafowl from a breeder near you.

While birds can adjust to different climates, finding birds from a breeder in your area will help prevent any problems from a climate change.

Bring the birds home in a secure peafowl container and try to make the trip as uneventful as possible. Don't fuss with the birds during transport and keep them in the back of an enclosed vehicle. Do not transport them in the back of a pickup truck as this can cause stress for the birds.

When the peafowl arrive home, place the container into the pen and place some food outside near the container. Carefully open the container and remove the tail wrappings from the bird. Do not rush and try to remain calm so you don't worry the bird.

Once the tail wrapping is off, step back and allow the peafowl to move out of the container on his own. Don't rush the bird at all.
When the bird is out exploring the pen on his own, remove the container and then leave the bird alone. During those first few days, try to keep the peafowl inside the stall and minimize the amount of contact you have with it. Feed and water the peafowl but simply coexist with it. Don't try to touch the bird or get too close unless there seems to be an illness occurring.

After a few days, you can begin to socialize with the bird a bit more but those first few days should be quiet, calm and free of a lot of outside stimulation.

By bringing your peafowl home properly, you are sure to have more success with your birds.

Chapter Six: Caring for Your Peacock

Although there is a lot of information throughout this book, caring for a peacock or any peafowl is really not that difficult. Peafowl do not require a lot of extra care and while you can spend a lot of time watching the birds, many take care of their own needs on a day-to-day basis.

In fact, outside of a proper diet, peafowl will deal with preening their feathers and can often go off on their own for longer periods of time, only checking in for their regular meal.

That being said, there are still some things that you should do to maintain the overall health of your bird. I will discuss feeding your peafowl in the next chapter, but in this chapter, I will go over the daily and yearly care involved in keeping your peafowl healthy.

1) Daily Care

As I have mentioned, you don't have to be as involved in daily care as you need to be with some other animals. It is important that you provide your peafowl with daily food, especially if they are penned, but I will go over feeding in the following chapter.

Examine the bird on a daily basis. Check to make sure that there are no unusual signs of illness and that your birds are alert and curious. If there is any listless behaviour or the birds seem off in either appearance or temperament, then it is important to bring the birds in to see a veterinarian.

Since most peafowl remain rather wary of their owners, it can be a bit difficult and unsettling for the bird to capture it each day for an examination, so I recommend that you merely carry out a visual examination. If you see something that makes you nervous, capture the bird and then do a physical examination before contacting your vet.

Once you have given your birds the daily visual examination, feed them. Peafowl should be fed twice per day, once in the early morning just after dawn and once in the early evening, just before sunset.

During the rest of the day, you can have a few treats for the birds but they will do most of their feeding during the start and the end of the day.

Water should be left out throughout the day and I should mention a few things about feeders and waterers. Firstly, you should never place your water in a drip style container that hangs above the bird. This can cause a lot of problems and affect the health of your bird.

Instead, use a bucket or pan where the water can rest on the ground. Make sure the container is not too large or you will find that your peafowl prefer to stand in the water instead of drink it.

With feed, place the grain mixture into an automatic feeder and mount it about 8 to 24 inches off the ground so the birds have easy access to it.

The remainder of the food, including the treats, can be placed on the ground or in pans on the ground. Like many other types of birds, peafowl like to scratch for the food so providing them with an opportunity to do so will also help avoid your birds becoming bored.

If your peafowl are free ranging, then you can keep cleaning the pens to a minimum and will only have to clean the pens when the birds are using it. I recommend that you keep a few pens available to your birds so they have somewhere to roost and also so you have somewhere for the birds if they are sick.

If the peafowl is kept in pens, try to tidy the pens on a daily basis and give it a good cleaning about once a week. Keep bedding clean.

One interesting fact to point out is that peafowl often "drop their droppings" when they are preening themselves and many have a preening site where they like to sit. Simply spray this area down once a day to keep the amount of bird droppings to a minimum.

The rest of the time, just remove feathers, which you can keep for decoration and also rake the dirt of the pen to keep the area clean and fresh. Place in straw for bedding to keep your peafowl comfortable.

And that is really all you need to do with the general care. Peafowl don't need to be bathed on a regular basis and will keep their feathers clean on their own.

2) Clipping the Wing

Before you decide to clip the wings of your peafowl, it is important to really make sure that it needs to be done. Birds use their wings for escape and while they can jump quite high, not being able to fly away for safety can leave them at risk of predation.

In addition, clipping is viewed as cruel by many in the peafowl world and some breeders may have specific recommendations regarding clipping their young birds.

If you decide to clip your bird's wings, you should be prepared to clip the wings every few months, usually every 2 to 3 months depending on individual bird and also on how short you cut the wing.

To trim the wings, follow these steps:

1. Make sure the bird is safe and won't get hurt. It is better to work with the bird on the ground.

2. Hold both of the legs and have an assistant stretch out the wing.

3. With sharp scissors, begin cutting the wing. The best way to do this is to follow the tertiary feathers, which are the inner flight feathers, as a guide.

4. Cut one feather at a time, following the tertiary feathers .

5. Clip until all the feathers on one wing are trimmed.

With peafowl, you should only clip one wing on the bird to prevent your birds from flying away. Once they are clipped, release the bird safely and then clip the next bird's wing.

3) Wormers and Vaccinations

Another task that you should do with your peafowl is to worm them. This is usually the only medication that you need to give your birds on a regular basis and it should be done about twice a year.

Wormers should be given once and then re-administered 10 days after the first treatment. There are many different types of wormers out there but I recommend that you use the wormers as directed by your veterinarian.

In addition to de worming your peafowl, it is important to have them vaccinated on a regular basis. Check with your vet to find out what diseases have been prevalent in the area so you are vaccinating against the right strains. At the end of this chapter, I have listed a number of diseases that your peafowl can be affected by and have indicated the ones where vaccinations can work as preventative care.

4) Administering Oral Medication

If you are worming your birds or have run into a situation where you need to administer oral medication, it is important to know how to properly administer it. If you do not administer the medication properly, you could risk your bird drowning in the medication or not receiving the proper amount.

To administer oral medication, follow these steps:

1. Catch the peafowl and have someone help you. Make sure the bird is held securely for both your safety and its own. It is better to work with the bird on the ground and hold onto both of the legs.

2. Once the bird is secure, carefully open the bird's mouth.

3. Have your assistant hold the top of the beak and place his fingers between the two parts of the beak to keep it opened for you to work.

4. Look inside the mouth. You will notice that there is a trachea tube at the base of the tongue. Make sure that you do not put the medication near that tube.

5. Fill a syringe (one that does not have a needle but has a very long and fine end) with the medication.

6. Insert the syringe in the mouth and push it down slightly so that it is just past the trachea opening. Be very careful when you do this to prevent injury.

7. Slowly press the plunger down.

8. Once the medication has been administered, remove the syringe from the bird's mouth. Let the bird open and close his mouth several times and watch him to make sure that the bird does not have any negative side effects from the medication.

9. After a few minutes, let the bird go.

5) Administering Intramuscular Medication

Although administering medication through a needle and syringe is often done by the vet, many peafowl owners eventually learn how to administer the medication themselves.

To administer oral medication, follow these steps:

1. Catch the peafowl and have someone help you.

2. Have the person hold the bird in his lap and place the bird on his back. Secure the wings against the person's body and with a free hand. Secure the bird's legs and knees with the other hand.

3. Once the bird is secure, find the breast muscle. This is done by running your fingers down the breast bone. The breast muscle is the firm flesh on either side of the breast bone.

4. When you know where the muscle is, fill the syringe with the medication. Make sure there are no air bubbles.

5. Insert the needle of the syringe into the breast bone, angling it 45° away from the breast bone. It is really important that you do not hit the breast bone as you could break the needle.

6. Press the plunger until all the medication has been administered.

7. Remove the needle, making sure that it is intact and then release the bird.

If you find that you need to give more than one shot, make sure that you administer it to both sides on alternate times.

6) Diseases

When it comes to illnesses, most breeders agree that peafowl are fairly healthy; however, this does not mean that they never get sick. It is important to be aware of the diseases that can affect the overall health of your birds to ensure that your peafowl remains healthy.

a) Viruses

Like all animals, peafowl are susceptible to some viruses. Some can be medicated while others cannot and will simply need to be treated.

Fowl Pox

Symptoms: Lesions on the skin, raised, crater like scars, conjunctiva in the eye.
Cause: Transmitted through the bite of mosquitoes infect with the virus.
Treatment: Topical creams for the lesions
Vaccination: Yes, can be administered before and during outbreak.

Newcastle Disease

Symptoms: Respiratory distress possibly resulting in death
Cause: Transmitted between birds.
Treatment: No treatment. The illness runs for 14 days. Vaccination has been successful at controlling the disease.
Vaccination: Yes, should be administered yearly.

Sinusitis

Symptoms: Sinuses in the eye swell.
Cause: Transmitted between hen and unborn chicks.
Treatment: No cure but antibiotics are used to treat the symptoms. All birds with Sinusitis are lifelong carriers and should not be bred.
Vaccination: No

Hemorrhagic Enteritis

Symptoms: Inflammation of the intestines, haemorrhaging in the intestines. High mortality rate. Usually affects birds between 4 to 13 weeks.
Cause: Transmitted between birds through faecal droppings.
Treatment: Antibiotics are used to treat the secondary infections caused by the disease but there is no

treatment for the disease itself. Clean pens and feed will help prevent the spread.
Vaccination: Yes, yearly vaccination can prevent the disease. Clean pens and sound husbandry will also prevent it.

Air Sacculitis

Symptoms: Inflamed air sacs and air reservoirs, excretion of pus from affected area.
Cause: Transmitted between hen and unborn chicks.
Treatment: No cure but antibiotics are used to treat the symptoms. All birds with Air Sacculitis are lifelong carriers and should not be bred.
Vaccination: No

M. synoviae

Symptoms: Inflamed joints, arthritis.
Cause: Transmitted between hen and unborn chicks.
Treatment: No cure but antibiotics are used to treat the symptoms. All birds with M. synoviae are lifelong carriers and should not be bred.
Vaccination: No

b) Bacteria

There are actually a number of bacteria that can be spread between birds, which can be very serious for your peafowl. In addition, some of the bacterial diseases can be spread between bird species so it is important to treat any diseases immediately.

Fowl Typhoid

Symptoms: Loss of appetite, dead eggs or chicks shortly after hatching, diarrhoea, drooping wings, and dehydration. Death of the bird.

Cause: Caused by the bacteria Salmonella gallinarum. Spread from parent birds to unhatched chicks.
Treatment: No cure, all birds that have been identified as having fowl typhoid are destroyed. Birds with the disease should not be bred.
Vaccination: No

Pullorum

Symptoms: Loss of appetite, dead eggs or chicks shortly after hatching, diarrhoea, drooping wings, and dehydration. Death of the bird.
Cause: Caused by the bacteria Salmonella pullorum. Spread from parent birds to unhatched chicks.
Treatment: No cure, all birds that have been identified as having fowl typhoid are destroyed. Birds with the disease should not be bred.
Vaccination: No

Arizona Infection

Symptoms: Loss of appetite, dead eggs or chicks shortly after hatching, and diarrhoea. High mortality rate.
Cause: Caused by the Arizona bacterium. Spread from parent birds to unhatched chicks.
Treatment: Neomycin and/or nitrofuran are used to treat and control the disease.
Vaccination: No

Avian Tuberculosis

Symptoms: Weight loss, decrease in egg production, diarrhoea, and increased thirst. Usually affects birds between the age of 3 and 4 years old.
Cause: Caused by the bacteria Mycobacterium avian. Spread from bird to bird through poor sanitation.
Treatment: No treatment. Prevention is done through proper sanitation and management of the aviary.
Vaccination: No

Paratyphoid

Symptoms: Trembling, diarrhoea, blindness, loss of appetite, weakness. Usually affects young chicks between the ages of 8 to 28 days and can result in death of the bird.

Cause: Caused by over 2000 serotypes of Salmonella bacteria. Spread from parent birds to chicks through the egg.
Treatment: Neomycin and/or nitrofuran are used to treat and control the disease
Vaccination: No

Fowl Cholera

Symptoms: Haemorrhaging, high mortality rate.
Cause: Caused by the bacteria *Pasteurella multocida*. Spread from bird to bird through poor sanitation.
Treatment: Treatment through sulfa drugs and antibiotics. Decontamination of the flock as well as the equipment and aviary needs to be done to prevent further infections.
Vaccination: Yes but not completely successful at preventing the disease.

Staphylococcus

Symptoms: Arthritis, septicema
Cause: Caused by the bacteria *Staphylococcus aureus* through poor sanitation in the environment.
Treatment: Treatment through antibiotics. Decontamination of the equipment and aviary needs to be done to prevent further infections.
Vaccination: No

c) Parasites

In addition to viruses and bacteria, peafowl and many other birds can become susceptible to various parasites. They can contract them from the environment or the parasites can be spread between birds.

In most cases, proper care and cleanliness of the aviary will help to prevent most of the parasites. For some, worming medications and treatments will help prevent and correct the problem.

Lice

Symptoms: Itching, restlessness, over preening
Cause: Lice are a small external parasite that eat skin, scales and feather debris. Spread from bird to bird and more commonly seen in peafowl that roam.
Treatment: Treatment with a pesticide. Make sure that treatment is bird safe.
Vaccination: No, treatment is the only way to deal with lice.

Gape Worms

Symptoms: Respiratory problems, secondary infections, respiratory distress.

Cause: A worm that moves into the trachea of the peafowl. Spread through improper hygiene in the pens and has been linked to earthworms as well.
Treatment: Treatment is done with Tramisol and/or Thiabendazole
Vaccination: No, de worming twice a year can help prevent.

Tapeworms

Symptoms: Weight loss, fragments of tapeworm in the faeces.
Cause: Spread through insects, crustaceans and arthropods, peafowl become infected by feeding from infected food.
Treatment: Treatment is done with worming medication.
Vaccination: No, de worming twice a year can help prevent.

Chiggers

Symptoms: Scabby lesions on the thighs, breast, vent and undersides of the wings.
Cause: Common mite that is found in the environment.
Treatment: Usually no treatment for the mite, which falls off after 14 days of feeding, however, the lesions are treated with medication.
Vaccination: No

Ascaridia Worms

Symptoms: Intestinal distress, diarrhoea, depressed state due to blood loss
Cause: A worm that moves through the intestinal tract of the peafowl. Spread through the environment and through faeces.
Treatment: Treatment is done with piperazine worm medicine.
Vaccination: No, de worming twice a year can help prevent.

Cecal Worms

Symptoms: Very few symptoms
Cause: Worms are spread from bird-to-bird. The cecal worm lives in the ceca of the peafowl.
Treatment: Treatment is done through wormers.
Vaccination: No, de worming twice a year can help prevent.

Capillaria Worms

Symptoms: Rough feathers, paleness, depressed state.
Cause: A worm that moves through the gastro-intestinal tract of the peafowl. Spread through the environment and from bird to bird.
Treatment: Treatment is done with wormers

Vaccination: No, de worming twice a year with Thiabendazole, Tramisol, Fenbandazole, or Ivermactin is important.

Mites

Symptoms: Itching, restlessness, over preening
Cause: Mites are a small external parasite that eat skin, scales and feather debris. Spread from bird to bird and more commonly seen in peafowl that roam.
Treatment: Treatment with a pesticide 3 or 4 times every 10 days. Make sure that treatment is bird safe.
Vaccination: No, treatment is the only way to deal with mites.

Chapter Seven: Feeding Your Peacock and Peafowl

Feeding your peafowl is not actually that difficult, since they thrive on common bird mixes that you would feed chickens or even wild birds. That being said, there are a few things that you should consider and in this chapter I will go over everything you need to know to properly feed your peafowl and peacocks.

1) The Basic Peafowl Diet

Before I get into depth about what you need to feed your peafowl, I should point out that there are many different opinions on what is best for your peafowl. The recommendations in this book are considered to be the best diet; however, peafowl can thrive on a variety of mixtures so I always recommend discussing diet with your peafowl breeder before you bring your bird home.

When it comes to looking at peafowl, owners should realize that peafowl are omnivores. This means that they eat seeds, vegetation and meat, or rather insects and do not solely eat manufactured foods. I will go over supplements later on in this chapter but when you are planning your diet, try to take their omnivorous diet into consideration.

Many peafowl breeders opt to feed their birds regular chicken feed. This is fine for many birds; however, it will not give them optimal feed and will not give them the proper nutrition.

Generally, if you are looking for food, you should choose a blend that is better formulated for other birds, or more specifically for quail. Although they are not a complete match, quail are very close to peafowl and their feed is much better for peafowl than any other type of feed.

That being said, you can also choose a chicken food. There are a few peafowl feeds available but they are fairly difficult to come by depending on where you live.

Regardless of the type of food that you use, it is important to add a bit more to the feed to ensure that your peafowl have optimal health. Here is what I recommend to ensure that your birds have a well blended diet.

- ***Quail Feed:*** The majority of your feed will be the quail feed and usually consists of a blend of seeds and grains that benefit the bird. It is important that you choose a quail feed that has kelp meal in it. Make sure that the kelp meal is raw and that it provides a high source of keratin. If the food does not, either order kelp meal and add about one part to two parts of feed to your food or find a different feed.

- ***Bird Seeds:*** Seeds are very important for your peafowl's diet and a blend of natural seeds and grains that are made for wild birds is a good choice. Choose one that is just a blend with a range of grains and seeds and does not have any fillers or preservatives. Organic and all natural products are the best for your birds.

When you combine these two feeds, use two parts quail feed and one part bird seed. Give the feed to your birds on a daily basis. The amount differs depending on several factors including:

- How many birds you have.
- If they are free ranging or if they are kept in a pen.
- Their age.
- The season.

Although the feed makes up a large part of their diet, you should never keep your peafowl on the feed alone. Peafowl have a large appetite and if they are free ranging birds you will find that they will usually cover many of the needs of their diet. However, if they live in a pen, especially if it is an earth floor pen, you will need to provide them with much of their ranging needs.

Regardless, there are a number of different items that you should offer your peafowl on a regular basis.

One: Meat

As I have mentioned, peafowl are omnivores so they do require some meat based protein in their diets. In fact, about 20% of the peafowl's diet should be protein. The best choice for this is a wet dog food.

Twice a week, break up two or three large cans of wet dog food. Simply toss it into the pen or around the area where your peafowl usually feed. The birds will scratch around for the food and will receive enough protein for the week.

When you choose dog food, choose a high quality one. Make sure that the dog food is free of soy, as this can affect the overall health of your birds.

Another source of meat can be worms or grubs. If you do purchase these, make sure that the insects are not invasive species as insects can get out of the pens. Simply toss the insects into the pen.

Two: Fruit

Although fruit is not usually added to the regular feed, it should be offered to your peafowl on a regular basis. This will help the birds get a well blended diet and will ensure that they get enough vitamins and minerals. One thing that you should note is that peafowl usually only dig through fruit for the seeds and don't usually eat it but some types of fruit they will eat.

Cut open the fruit so the peafowl can get at the soft fruit and seeds inside. You can also cut it into very small bits and toss it into the pen so the peafowl can scratch for it. If you do this, make sure that you consider the size of their beaks so the food is not too difficult for them to swallow.

Some types of fruit that peafowl like are:

- ***Melons:*** Any type of melon is a good choice for peafowl. Make sure you cut this open and just set it in the pen. The peafowl will do the rest.

- ***Berries:*** Ranging peafowl will often find berries to eat on their own but blueberries, raspberries and strawberries can be a nice treat for the birds.

- ***Grapes:*** Many peafowl will eat the whole fruit.

- ***Citrus Fruit***: Again, cut citrus fruit open and simply leave them out for the birds to eat.

- ***Pumpkin:*** Pumpkin has often been identified as a natural wormer and is an excellent choice during the winter.

Three: Greens and Vegetables

If you have the ability to do this, try to keep grass growing in your pens since peafowl will eat snippets of the grass and you won't need to add a lot of different vegetables and greens to their diet.

If you can't keep grass growing in the pens, which can be very difficult, make sure that you offer your peafowl greens and some types of vegetables. Again, most of these do not need to be broken down but simply cut open in the case of hard shelled vegetables. Make sure you offer vegetables two or three times a week.

- ***Plants:*** You can offer plant snippings. I have provided you with a list of plants and flowers that peafowl find appetizing in the section on range feeding.
- ***Lettuce:*** Lettuce and other green leafy vegetables are good for peafowl.
- ***Squash:*** Like pumpkins, squash is an excellent winter treat and it can be used as a natural wormer.

Four: Grains

While your peafowl will receive a fair amount of their grain intake in their feed, you can also offer them breads, rice and other grain products throughout the year. This provides them with variety and the birds enjoy getting treats.

In addition to these foods, you can also offer things like cheese to your peafowl and there really aren't too many restrictions.

In fact, the more variety you have in your peafowl's diet, the better your peafowl's health will be. This will translate into happier birds that have better colouring and will also help your bird's fertility.

When you feed your birds, remember that peafowl usually forage for food in the early morning and late afternoon, usually right before sunset. Plan to feed your birds at this time.

2) Range Feeding

If we are looking at range feeding peafowl, you aren't going to make a lot of changes to the overall diet. Generally, the range feeding birds will have access to all the extra foods; however, you want to make sure that you offer the same opportunities for fruit, meat and vegetables.

The main difference is that you will need to find an ideal spot to feed your range feeding birds as opposed to the ones kept in a pen.

When a peacock or peafowl is free ranging, they have a wide variety of food available to them. Although their primary diet is seeds and the quail feed that you provide them, they will also eat insects, small animals and even snakes. In fact, peafowl will eat just about anything and they can even eat poisonous snakes.

Peafowl will also eat plants that you have in and around your property. Be sure to fence off or screen your gardens as peafowl will find their way into them. While they may focus on the bugs, some of your flowers and plants may seem too tempting to leave alone so be prepared for them to be eaten.

Another point that you should consider is a free ranging bird will forage away from your property so make sure that your surrounding neighbours are okay with having a peacock eating their plants.

One thing that you should be aware of is that peafowl are often described as the goat of the bird world. They will eat just about anything so make sure that your yard is free of manmade hazards. Things like Styrofoam pellets, plastic caps and small pieces of fabric can all be ingested by the birds and will make them sick or result in death.

For the rest, let your birds take care of their feeding and you will find that by providing enough variety to your regular feed, on top of what they are foraging, that your birds will be healthy and happy with a splendid display of colour.

Plants Peafowl Eat

Below is a list of plants that peafowl enjoy eating. Make sure that you offer a few of these plants as having more foraging in your own yard and garden will keep the peafowl on your property more.

- ***Seedlings:*** First, any type of young plant or seedling is a popular treat for ranging peafowl. If you have a few plants that you want to keep safe, cover them until they are large enough so that the peafowl will ignore them.

- ***Flowers:*** Flowers are not actually eaten but tend to be decimated for various reasons. The bird may be looking for insects or looking for seeds. Sometimes, peafowl will simply destroy a flower out of boredom. While any type of flower can fall prey to a peafowl, some that they really enjoy are:

  - Amaryllis
  - Begonia
  - Impatiens
  - Pansy
  - Petunia
  - Primrose

- ***Vegetables:*** While a garden can be a wonderful place for your peafowl to roam since there is an abundance of bugs, they will also devour some of your vegetables. Some vegetables that they eat are:
  - Brussels Sprouts
  - Cabbage
  - Cauliflower
  - Chives
  - Lettuce
  - Tomato
  - Spinach

- ***Berry Plants:*** Any type of berry plant will catch your peafowl's interest but they are fond of Holly and also Blackberry and Blueberry.

3) Supplements

When it comes to supplementing your peafowl's diet, there really isn't much that you need to add. Remember that a diet that is full of variety will have enough vitamins and minerals in the food to make sure that the birds stay healthy.

Before you decide whether to give your peafowl additional vitamins and minerals, make sure you speak with your veterinarian. Follow his recommendations. If you do not use vitamins and minerals, make sure the following foods are available to your peafowl on a regular basis to ensure they get everything they need.

- ***Bamboo Shoots:*** Purchase canned bamboo as it is softer. These are full of minerals and vitamins. Feed one to three times per week.

- ***Banana:*** The older the banana, the better, but bananas are a good source of potassium. Feed half a banana per bird, soaked, twice a week.

- ***Celery:*** Feed celery to your peafowl about 5 times per week. Celery has been linked to a better digestive system in peafowl.

- ***Chickpeas:*** Do not feed your peafowl manufactured chickpeas, instead, soak the chickpeas on your own and add them to the daily feed or use them as a treat. One cup of chickpeas offers your bird enough minerals to cover the daily suggested amount and have 10 different vitamins to increase their health.

- ***Frogs Legs:*** Peafowl will often eat small lizards and amphibians when they are foraging and you can offer them frogs legs once a week for an alternative to their protein intake.

- ***Kale:*** Raw kale is bursting with vitamins and is a good source of fibre for your birds. Try to offer a cup of minced kale every day.

- ***Mushrooms:*** Again, these are full of minerals and vitamins and you should try to feed your peafowl mushrooms about one to three times per week.

- ***Shrimp:*** Make sure the shrimp has its shell since it is the shell that you want your peafowl to eat. The amino acids in the shrimp will help with digestion. Offer your birds two or three shrimp per week.

- ***Sweet Potato:*** Cook the sweet potato and offer it to the birds in its skin once a week. It is rich in vitamins and minerals .

- ***Walnuts:*** Walnuts are an excellent source of vitamin E and should be fed twice a week. Only feed about two walnut pieces per bird.

In addition to these supplements to your peafowl's diet, make sure you offer your peafowl fresh water every day and try to place the water on the ground. Hanging waterers are not appropriate for peafowl.

Lastly, make sure your peafowl has an opportunity to eat gravel from time to time to help with their digestion.

4) Feeding Peachicks

In general, there isn't much that you need to do with your peachicks when it comes to feeding. Peahens are very good mothers and will often take over the care of the chicks at an early stage.

For their diet, I do recommend that you start the peachicks on a quail starter diet or a turkey starter diet. You can then place them on a grower feed but generally, if you follow a diverse diet for your peafowl, you really don't need to make too many accommodations for the young.

By three days old, the peachicks will begin to forage on their own and during this time, make sure you offer them a larger quantity of meat and protein based foods. After a few weeks they will begin to eat more greens and grains but during the initial growth their diet will consist of a high protein level. You should try to offer them a diet where 30% of their daily feed is protein based and then slowly reduce it down to the 20% by the time they are a few months old.

While it does seem like there is a lot to do with feeding your peafowl, really, it is not that difficult and you can simply place the food out for the birds. If you use more of the supplements for your birds, make sure that you also remove some of the empty calories. Things like bread and cheese aren't really needed and it is better to fill up your bird's diet with the healthier selections.

Chapter Eight: Socializing your Peacock and Peafowl

One area that is often up for debate is whether or not you really need to socialize your peacocks or peafowls. As I have mentioned several times throughout this book, peafowl are usually very standoffish birds and they don't really bond with their owners.

That being said, I have always felt that socializing your peafowl is just as important as socializing your dog. Peafowl that understand that you are not a threat are more likely to stay within sight of you and you will be able to enjoy them much more than if they stay hidden.

1) Creating a Friendlier Peafowl

The first thing that I should point out is that you should never expect to have a peacock or a peafowl that will come and sit on your lap and spend the day with you. There are the occasional stories about peafowl that are very friendly; however, these peafowl are few and far between.

Generally, the best that most breeders achieve is a bird that will simply keep a three to five foot distance from humans and often that is close enough to truly enjoy the beauty of a peacock.

To promote this type of socialization, it is better to start with the bird as a chick:

- ***Hold it often.*** Make sure that you hold the chick on a daily basis, several times per day.

- ***Place it where there is human contact.*** Although you may not want it in the house, have the peachick as close to humans as possible so it rests and spends its day next to people.

- ***Hand feed the chick.*** Always feed the chick by hand. Like most animals, the more it sees you as a positive thing, such as a place to get food, the more likely it will come to you when it is older.

- ***Avoid corrections.*** Unlike a dog, a peachick is not going to learn commands and training. Remember that these are semi-wild animals and they will behave as such. Correcting the bird for doing something you view as wrong will only make the bird wary of you and the bird will avoid coming close.

One thing that should be mentioned is that this type of socialization can be both a positive and negative thing. On one hand, you may get a very tame peafowl that will even come up and perch on you. On the other hand, there have been cases of peafowl becoming aggressive to humans after socialization. The main reason why this occurs is because the bird starts to view you as one of its own species. Once it does this, it will start to view you as competition to its territory.

Peahens are usually much better to socialize than peacocks as they tend to be less agressive.

If you are purchasing an older bird, it is important to do your research. Make sure some socialization went into the raising of the bird.

Even if it did, you will need to take the time to really get to know the bird and get it to trust you. Always do this with food. Keep treats on hand and gradually throw the food closer to you so the birds needs to come closer to get the treat. Eventually, the bird will feel comfortable eating closer to you and will not view you as a threat to them.

2) Keeping your Peafowl at Home

One part of socialization that is very important for your peafowl is conditioning them so that they stay at home. Peafowl will roam quite far if they can so those first few weeks when you bring your peafowl home is very important for their socialization.

Although this can be done successfully with older peafowl, the ideal is a peafowl that is about a year old. Older peafowl will have a harder time being conditioned to your home and some never are. If you purchase older peafowl, I recommend that you keep them penned or take even longer to properly condition them.

The main reason to choose yearling peafowl is because the birds are hardier than chicks and will have fewer threats from predators. In addition, they have not been conditioned to other places yet so there is less chance of the bird getting confused.

When you bring your birds home, place them into an inside pen. You want to make sure that the birds have places to roost that are 3 to 4 feet above the ground and that it is in an enclosed space where the birds will be safe.

Before you place them into the pen, clip their wings as it will make them less likely to try to fly to get out. Give them plenty of food and make sure they see that it is you feeding them every time.
Once they have been in the inside pen for a month, you can begin to bring them outside into a flight pen. The best way to do this is to simply have a covered flight pen attached to the inside pen. The birds can go in and out as they choose.

Continue to keep them inside the enclosure for another month and remember to give them plenty of treats so they become less nervous about having you around them every day.

After the confinement time has passed, open the enclosure door and leave it open during the day. Do not go in and flush them from the pen but instead let them come out of it on their own. Monitor the birds during this time to make sure that nothing happens to them.

Allow them to roam close to the enclosure for a few hours each day, lengthening the time that you do, and then herd them back into the enclosure. Always make sure that they are locked in safe during the night.

Continue this until the peafowl can be left out for the majority of the day. Every night, try to round them up and place them into their enclosure to keep them safe. Do this for several months.

Once you know you can trust the birds to stay fairly close to their enclosure, or at least come back to it fairly quickly, you can begin to leave the peafowl out throughout the night. Personally, I prefer to get them in at night but this cannot always be helped.

Throughout all of this, it is very important for you to continue socializing the birds to you and to give them plenty of treats so they do not become fearful.

3) Peafowl and Pets

Despite the fact that there can be some predation from other pets, peafowl tend to get along with most pets. They are fairly calm and the only time when they will be aggressive is if they are feeling threatened.

Special care needs to be taken with peafowl and dogs since many dogs will chase the birds. Train your dogs to ignore the peafowl and correct the dog, not the bird.

If you find that you cannot train your dog to ignore the peafowl, then you will have to make the decision to keep the peafowl penned for their own safety. In addition, peafowl will defend against dogs if they are placed in a flight or fight situation and both the birds and dog can be injured if this happens.

In addition to dogs, you should be careful with cats, especially when you have chicks. Generally, the peafowl will chase off cats but when the chicks are under 4 weeks old they are at a higher risk for predation so make sure that you keep them safe from the cats.

During the rest of the year, the peafowl will usually do fine with any type of pet but you should watch during the first few interactions with your other pets.

Socializing your birds can be very easy to do and usually all it takes is plenty of food and a calm demeanour so the bird will begin to trust you.

Chapter Nine: Nesting and Breeding

For many people, breeding peafowl becomes a hobby that they never intended to get into. The main reason for having a peafowl was simply to enjoy the birds and the eggs and breeding simply came as a result of owning both peacocks and peahens.

Left on their own, peafowl will multiply quite quickly if they are given the proper food and care during the months. In fact, many free ranging birds will produce their own peachicks without your aid and you can often be surprised by the sudden appearance of the young.

For those that are not free ranging, you will have to plan out your breeding to ensure that you get exactly what you want. In this chapter, I will go over everything you need to know about hatching and raising your own peachicks.

1)Breeding

The very first step to breeding peafowl is to select the proper birds for the laying season. Generally, most species of peafowl are mature by 2 years of age, but some have been known to produce eggs by a year. Although you can get eggs from some birds at 1 year old, I strongly recommend that you wait until the peahens are 2 or 3 years of age.

With males, never try to breed them until they are 2 years of age and it is often better to wait until they are 3 years of age. Some peafowl, including the green peafowls, take longer to mature so don't worry if your peafowl are not producing until they are older.

When you are choosing your breeding stock, there are a few things you should look for.

1. ***Overall Health:*** The birds should appear healthy. Eyes should be clear, firm flesh and musculature, bright feathers, alert and curious. If they are not, you may have an illness in your birds that should be addressed first.
2. ***Colour:*** Choose birds that have a colour or trait that you want to reproduce. While all peacocks can be beautiful, some are truly majestic and will have traits you want to pass down to young.

3. ***Temperament:*** Although this isn't usually as important as health, you will want to have a peacock with good temperament. The more aggressive a peacock is, the better a breeder he is. You want a peacock with a good aggression level but not so aggressive that he makes it difficult for you to get in and manage your peafowl.

With all of your breeding stock, take the time to have health tests done. If you have not read it, read the chapter on caring for your birds to determine what health problems are transferred to the chicks. It can be devastating to watch all of your peachicks succumb to an illness.

Once you have all the proper clearances and you have decided on the birds, you simply need to place them into pens together.

Mating starts in early spring and a male peacock can be placed with about 5 peahens and produce a good clutch of eggs.

All new breeders should note that usually the first year of laying is a small clutch; however, the second year is much larger.

2) *Laying*

Laying usually begins sometime in April and the peahen will produce a number of eggs throughout the spring and summer months.

Generally, a hen will roost and then lay the eggs or she will lay the eggs onto the grounds. Do not be worried if she lays the eggs from a height of about 4 feet off the ground as the eggs will usually survive a fall of that distance.

What you do need to worry about is the eggs falling onto debris, including droppings. Under the roosting area, place straw or hay so the eggs have something soft to land on. In addition, keep the area very clean and remove any debris or faeces on a daily basis.

If you are allowing the peahen to set on the eggs herself, you should expect 2 clutches of eggs at the most over the spring and summer months. Generally, a peahen will lay 5 to 10 eggs in each clutch, although occasionally you will see larger clutches.

If you are incubating the eggs, then the peahen will usually produce eggs every other day for the entire breeding season, usually up to about 30 eggs, although some produce more. You may find that occasionally she will have a few days without production but generally she will start up again after a few days.

3) Incubation

Now that the eggs are laid, it is time for incubation. As I have mentioned, if the peahen is setting on the eggs herself, then you should only expect 1 to 2 clutches of eggs.

Incubation for peafowl is between 27 to 29 days and it can vary depending on the species, which is included in a chart at the end of this section.

If you decide to incubate the eggs using an incubator, then you will need to plan for this. Make sure that you have a high quality incubator for your eggs as well as a hatcher.

Before breeding season, prepare your incubators. Clean them thoroughly so there is no chance of cross contamination from previous years. In addition, set the incubator in a room where you have a consistent temperature. Although the incubator has its own environment, placing it in a room that is too cold or too hot can affect the hatching.

Next, set up the incubator so that it has a temperature of about 99 to 100°F. If you can, purchase a model with an air circulation fan to ensure the temperature stays even. You should also check the temperature in several spots on your incubator to make sure there is an even distribution of heat.

One tip that works really well for incubation is to have the door of the incubator open slightly. This allows fresh air to pass through the incubator and it is very important for the development of the peachicks.

Another important part of incubation is to have the proper humidity levels. Generally, humidity should be at about 80 to 88% and the humidity level should be adjusted to accommodate that. Purchase a hygrometer, which gauges the humidity, and take into account that the humidity in the room that may affect the incubator.

Once the incubator is ready and the peahens are laying their eggs, you can start collecting the eggs. Some points to remember when collecting are:

- ***Do not stack too many eggs together.*** The weight of the top eggs can crush the bottom eggs so only make the depth three or four eggs deep.

- ***Mark each egg.*** When collecting from multiple pens, number the pens and then write the number on each of the eggs with pencil. Do not use markers as the ink can seep through the egg shell and kill the growing chick. Mark the egg in several locations so you don't have to worry about the number rubbing off.

- ***Date the eggs.*** Remember to place a date on each egg as well or have a chart where you assign numbers to the date collected and pens. This will help keep things in order.

- ***Search through the pen.*** Some peahens will cover up their eggs when they hatch them so make sure you thoroughly search through the pen.

Once you get the eggs, look through them and remove any that have been cracked when the peahen was laying them. For the rest, you can either wait to put them in the incubator or set them in.

If you choose to wait, keep the eggs at 55 to 60°F with no humidity. You can hold them for about 7 days after laying but never wait longer than that or you will not have a viable egg after that time.

For the ones that go into incubator, place them on their sides in the incubator tray and point the tip downwards slightly.

As the eggs are incubating, it is very important to maintain the humidity and the temperature. In addition, the eggs should be turned every 2 to 2 hours by about 45° for proper development.

During incubation time, candle the eggs about once a week to check for fertility. Eggs that have no signs of fertility for 10 days should be removed as they will not develop into chicks. To candle an egg:

1. Place a bare light bulb with a drop cord inside a cardboard box.

2. Cut a hole in the cardboard box that is about ½ an inch in diameter.

3. Seal the rest of the box.

4. Turn off the light in the room if possible.

5. Take an egg and holding it on the top and bottom, place it against the hole so the light shines through the egg. You should be able to see the yolk and the chick depending on the stage of development.

If an egg is infertile, you will simply see a clear egg and a shadow where the yolk is. This is an egg that should be removed from the incubator, although you should wait at least 10 days before you remove it.

A fertilized egg should have a spider like shape in the candled egg. This is the embryo and the blood vessels moving out from it.

An egg where the embryo has died is called a dead germ egg and when this occurs, you will see the spider like embryo but you will also see a ring of blood around the embryo. This is caused by the blood moving away from the embryo after death. Any dead germ eggs should be removed.

Eggs that are fertile should go back to incubation and as the peachick develops you may start seeing the chick form and possibly move inside the egg.

Peafowl Breed	Incubation Time	Stop Turning
Indian Blue Peafowl	27 to 29 days	25th day
Green Peafowl	28 days	26th day
Other Peafowl	27 to 29 days	25th day

4) Hatching

Hatching usually begins between 27 to 29 days after the eggs have been set on but before that occurs there is a very important step that breeders should take and that is not turning the eggs.

Generally, the eggs are moved to a hatcher when they are 25 to 26 days in incubation. Temperature levels in the hatcher should be kept at the same 99 to 100°F level but the humidity should be raised slightly, usually keeping it closer to 88%.

The eggs should not be turned during this time as turning will prevent the chick from orienting itself for hatching.

After two or three days in the hatcher, the chicks will begin to hatch. It is important to leave the chick in the hatcher for an additional day after hatching to give it time to stand up on its own and begin moving around.

5) Young Peachicks

Caring for your young peachicks can be fairly simple and it really depends on whether or not you are raising the chicks on your own.

If your peafowl set the eggs herself, then simply leave the peachicks with her. She will see that they are getting fed and will keep them safe. Although some breeders disagree, in most cases, peahens are amazing mothers. The only real concern that you should take is keeping the peachicks safe from predators since peahens nest on the ground. The best way to do this is to keep the peahens penned during nesting.

If the peachicks are incubated in an incubator, then you will need to do a bit more work with them.

After they have been hatched, remember to let the peachick stay in the hatcher for an extra day. Once that time has passed, move the peachick to a brooder that has a similar temperature and humidity level as the hatcher.

One thing that I strongly recommend is to have several brooders. This way you can move the peachicks to a different room as they age so they stay with other peachicks their size. This prevents younger peachicks from not being injured and you can slowly decrease the temperature from room to room.

Keep the peachicks inside the brooders for roughly 10 weeks, although I recommend trying to keep them in the brooders for about 12 weeks.

During that time, clean the brooders on a daily basis to prevent diseases in your peachicks. In addition, make sure there is a constant supply of fresh, clean water for the peachicks to drink.

Start the peachicks on a starter feed and I recommend you read the chapter on peafowl diet to learn how to feed a peachick. However, start feeds should be stopped once the peachick is 6 months of age.

Once they are twelve weeks of age, you can begin moving them into juvenile pens and then finally allow them access to an outdoor pen. Do not allow a peachick to roam before it is a year old and has been properly conditioned.

Chapter Ten: Common Terms

If you are interested in raising and breeding your own peafowl, then it is important to understand the various terms that you will become accustomed to in the bird raising world.

Aviary: A cage, pen or other enclosure where a bird is kept. Can also refer to a farm where birds are bred.

Avian Veterinarian: An animal doctor who specializes in the care of birds.

Beak: This is the beak of the peafowl.

Clutch: A grouping of eggs that have been laid at the same time by the same hen.

Endangered: Something that is threatened and close to extinction.

Eyespot: A spot that is eyelike, which is found on the train of a male peafowl.

Feed: The grain food that is fed to animals.

Free range: A bird that is allowed to roam on a property and is not caged or penned.

Hatcher: A machine that artificially warms the eggs. Used right before hatching.

Hatching: When the peachick emerges from the egg.

Incubation: The process of providing heat, humidity and movement for the healthy development of an embryo in an egg.

Incubator: A machine where eggs are incubated by means of artificial heat, humidity and movement.

Iridescence: A shimmery spectrum of colours.

Laying: The act of producing eggs.

Moulting: When feathers are shed. Usually occurs yearly after breeding season.

Ocilli: A spot that is eyelike, which is found on the train of a male peafowl.

Peachick: A young, or baby, peafowl.

Peacock: The male peafowl.

Peafowl: Any bird that is from the Genera Pavo that originated in Sri Lanka, India, and South-eastern Asia.

Peahen: The female peafowl.

Pen: An enclosure where a bird is kept.

Predator: An animal that hunts and attacks other animals. Preys upon peafowl.

Preening: When a bird cleans its feathers.

Quail: A small game bird.

Roosting: A perch where birds can sit or rest upon.

Set/Setting: The act of sitting on eggs for incubation.

Sex: To determine the gender of the bird.

Tail: The tail of the bird consists of roughly 20 feathers. In males, the train is attached to the tail.

Train: The long tail that is seen on male peafowl. It consists of roughly 200 feathers that make up the impressive display.

Wormers: Medications used to treat or prevent internal parasites.

Yearling: A peafowl that is a year old.

Photo Credits:

© Newphotoservice | Dreamstime.com

:© Micha Fleuren | Dreamstime.com

© F9photos | Dreamstime.com

© Mark Karasek | Dreamstime.com

© Anna Maria Simonini | Dreamstime.com

© Petr Jilek | Dreamstime.com

© Michalowski | Dreamstime.com

© Mikefoto | Dreamstime.com

© Boris Fojtik | Dreamstime.com

© Eric Gevaert | Dreamstime.com

© Worradirek Muksab | Dreamstime.com

:© Vladimir Hroch | Dreamstime.com

© Musat Christian | Dreamstime.com

© Rodolfo Arpia | Dreamstime.com

© Arindom Chowdhury | Dreamstime.com

© Rjsalinas | Dreamstime.com

© Trevor Payne | Dreamstime.com

© Sunheyy | Dreamstime.com

© Michal Durinik | Dreamstime.com

Notes:

Notes:

Lightning Source UK Ltd.
Milton Keynes UK
UKHW02f1953030918
328269UK00006B/312/P

9 780956 626998